PRIMAL SCREAM

An illustrated biography
by Stuart Coles

 OMNIBUS PRESS

Chapter One

"Punk music gave me the courage to be myself and I met Alan (McGee) through that.
I'd always thought that there must be people who think like me and when I heard 'God Save The Queen'
I thought, 'Great, there's somebody else who hates the Queen as much as I do'.
It's simple, but that's the power of rock 'n' roll!"

Bobby Gillespie

As a child of the Sixties, Bobby Gillespie's childhood musical diet was dominated by The Beatles, but the Glasgow born and bred youngster rapidly developed a preference for rockier groups such as The Who and The Rolling Stones. While on the surface the Fab Four were squeaky clean, Bobby preferred the undercurrent of anarchy and rebellion that the other two groups displayed.

By the time his teen years were nearly on him, this obsession with music had broadened and he was now steeped in the work of a whole host of musicians from across the world - George Clinton and P-Funk, classic Memphis soul, Gram Parsons, Dan Penn and Merle Haggard to name but a few. Then, in 1976, when Bobby was 13, his fascination with the more excessive side of rock 'n' roll found a perfect focus with the arrival of punk. While much of Britain was repelled by the antics of this new movement, Bobby became obsessed. He befriended Alan McGee who was two years above him at school and who also loved punk. The Sex Pistols were their obvious heroes, but they devoured the music and lifestyle of The Clash, Buzzcocks, and all punk's bastard children with relish.

Inspired like thousands of others by the DIY ethic that lay at the very core of punk rock, the two friends began to scour the music papers for band adverts with the aim of forming their own group. In this way they met Andrew Innes, with whom they formed a very loose trio, as Alan McGee later recalled in *Record Collector*, "We used to go round and drink beer at Andrew Innes's and Bobby used to roll around and just scream! We had like four rehearsals. That's January 1978."

At this stage, Bobby was in fact the least involved of the three, as McGee and Innes could actually play guitars, whereas he could only (barely) sing. Calling themselves a host of appalling names, such as The Drains and Captain Scarlet & The Mysterons, the fledgling band's career was inevitably doomed, but this was the first paving stone on the long and turbulent path towards Primal Scream. In the years between this shambolic start and Bobby's later elevation to near-iconic status, there were a myriad of personnel changes and problems with his band, but the core of Primal Scream has always been Bobby Gillespie.

After only a few weeks with Captain Scarlet & The Mysterons, Bobby faded out of the picture, leaving Innes and McGee to join forces with Neil Clarke (later of Lloyd Cole And The Commotions), and rename themselves first H_2O, then Newspeak and finally The Laughing Apple. After deciding that Glasgow did not offer them the chances to break through into the big time, McGee and Innes moved wholesale to London. Once there, McGee became immersed in the independent record scene and filled his cheap digs with dozens of underground fanzines (he wrote two issues of his own publication, entitled *Communication Blur*). He even ran his own club, where he encouraged and booked unknown alternative acts. After a few ill-fated recordings with The Laughing Apple and more failed band line-ups, McGee turned his restless energies to forming a record label. With his friend Joe Foster, formerly of The TV Personalities, McGee set up Creation in 1984.

Bobby, now 16, was only just leaving school. He worked briefly in a print shop, but soon bored of the nine-to-five life and put his new-found knowledge to good use by helping McGee with his early Creation artwork (including some impressive Laughing Apple designs). In the evenings Bobby teamed up with a friend called Jim Beattie and together they rehearsed in the local scout hall, playing what amounted to little more than untrained white noise. They even used an old ventilator and a couple of dustbin lids. At this stage, their guitar skills restricted them to playing rudimentary covers. "We were completely dissonant," Bobby later told Ann Scanlon of *Sounds*. "It wasn't music, it was just fucking smashing stuff up and screaming with guitars. We just used to make tapes of noises, then we found a few chords on the guitar and learnt songs like 'Mr Tambourine Man', 'Waiting For The Man' and 'Heroin'. Then I thought I could do some songs myself, so I started writing my own tunes and suddenly we had a pop group!" Inspired by the title of a 1970 book by Dr Arthur Janov about the anguished howls that emerge from psychotherapy clinics, Bobby and Jim christened themselves Primal Scream.

The first Primal Scream gig that Bobby recalls was at The Bungalow Bar in Paisley, as he told *Record Collector*, "We supported The Laughing Apple, only one song in the set was ours, and I remember it was just total noise. That wasn't a real gig, it was a joke. There wasn't any shape to it." Bobby also kept busy by playing occasional guitar and keyboard for fellow Glaswegians The Wake, even contributing lyrics to one track entitled 'The Old Men' which surfaced on a promotional video they recorded for the track 'Uniforms'.

This shambolic live start did not get much better with practice - gigs in and around the local scene followed, but there was no real substance (or talent) to these early Primal Scream shows. This rather crude ability was reflected in the band's first recorded output, a 1984 cassette taken from the *Pleasantly Surprised* series which showcased two tracks, 'State of Affairs' and 'Intro', both of which were awash in noise and devoid of structure. Ironically, before Primal Scream could establish their own identity, Bobby joined one of alternative rock's most influential bands of the Eighties, The Jesus & Mary Chain, the brainchild and obsession of brothers Jim and William Reid.

Bobby first heard the Reids' peculiar and highly idiosyncratic blend of noise, melody and guitar effects on the B-side of a collection of Syd Barrett songs given to him by a friend. The swathes of guitar feedback and punchy pop tunes captivated him, so he contacted the two brothers and told them to send a tape to his friend McGee at Creation. McGee was dazzled by the demo and signed the band almost immediately.

The Mary Chain's fleeting but brilliant live shows soon began to fascinate the London music scene, and the rock press hailed this great new talent. Bobby attended as many of these early shows as he could, and was therefore particularly delighted to find at one gig that the band's original drummer had left. Although he was barely competent on the skins, Bobby offered to help them out until a more permanent replacement was found. All this time, Primal Scream were still developing, but for now Bobby was obsessed with The Mary Chain. The liaison had its advantages - when The Mary Chain played gigs, such as the one at Glasgow's The Venue, Primal Scream were offered a support slot. Many observers class this particular gig, on October 11, 1984, as the actual start of Primal Scream as we know them today. As with many gigs to come during this period, Bobby played the support slot with his own band, and then climbed back up on stage to stand behind a solitary snare drum for The Mary Chain.

Shortly after this show, The Mary Chain released their Creation début, 'Upside Down', toured triumphantly throughout Europe and put out the seminal and critically revered début album *Psychocandy*. A performance on *The Whistle Test* and a major label deal followed, all with Bobby still on the drums.

Concerned that his new-found band would take away the focus from Primal Scream, Bobby and the band recorded a demo tape of four tracks rich with pop melodies, including the beautiful 'We Go Down Slowly Rising'. It was the first inkling of the great things to come from Primal Scream. Having signed, not unexpectedly, to Creation, Primal Scream quickly released their own début single entitled 'All Fall Down' backed with 'It Happens', both of which were a welcome change from the current musical vogue for Goth rock by the all-conquering Mission and The Sisters of Mercy. The first of many Primal Scream personnel changes took place when they fleshed their sound out with a rhythm guitarist and percussionist. Away from the rehearsals, and inspired by McGee's own work, Bobby also helped promote the Splash One club in Glasgow as a showcase for struggling alternative bands around the city.

With a second single under their belts, the disappointing 'Crystal Crescent', Primal Scream's career began to gather momentum, aided by Bobby's departure from his temporary role as The Mary Chain's drummer. As Bobby told *Record Collector*, "I never really enjoyed being in Primal Scream... but The Mary Chain is Jim and William's band and I knew I could express myself better in Primal Scream." It was now early 1986.

The band's second single was something of an anti-climax, but the B-side had suddenly begun to arouse interest in Primal Scream. Entitled 'Velocity Girl', it was a sub-90 second romp through rock, punk, and pop. The *NME* picked up on the track and included it on their influential *C86* cassette which was given away free with the magazine and contained a string of new bands, including The Wedding Present, and McCarthy. The bands featured played gigs in and around London on the back of the tape's success, including a show at The ICA. Even John Peel was impressed, placing 'Velocity Girl' at No. 4 in his revered "Festive 50" listings. Still later, the B-side was noted as the inspiration for The Stone Roses' classic 1989 single 'Made Of Stone'.

Interviewed at the time by *Zig Zag* magazine, Bobby and Jim Beattie were suitably obtuse about their hopes, despite this flurry of interest. Bobby started off by talking about his favourite things to do, saying he loved "Films, sometimes, flowers, trees. I think some trees remind me of people's haircuts. I really like trees." Jim was equally shadowy, saying "I'd like to earn enough money to buy a castle, I'd like to live in a castle. Not for a pose... no, I really like castles." When Bobby finally started talking sense, he gave a prosaic summary of the band's progress thus far: "We used to make noises, then we learnt to play guitars, then we learnt to write songs, and we quite liked it, and we thought, 'We'll try and get a group, try and get records out and things like that.'" Curiously, even at this early stage, *Zig Zag* were suitably impressed, finishing the interview with the prophetic "I'll give Primal Scream a good few years more than most."

Chapter Two

"If you've got a brain then you're OK with drugs,
It's like a motor car, you can kill yourself with

a car if you drive wrongly.
Give people the choice, that's what I say."

Bobby Gillespie

The band's thoughts now turned towards their début
album. Despite Creation's fragile financial status, the
Scream's sessions at the plush residential Rockfield
Studios in Wales cost a whopping £40,000 and were an
unmitigated disaster. Producer Stephen Street, who
would later to come to fame for shaping Blur's Britpop
masterpiece *Parklife*, saw all his work abandoned as
Primal Scream chose instead to start from scratch with a
new producer Mayo Thompson, formerly of the weird
experimentalists Red Krayola.

The first single from these sessions was 'Gentle Tuesday', which was released in June of 1987 and enjoyed a promo video airing on ITV's *The Chart Show*. Jim Beattie's Byrds influences were clearly at the fore on this record, with its jangly guitar and snatches of Sixties rock. When Andrew Innes re-joined that summer, alongside new recruit and future mainstay Robert Young (aka "Throb"), the second single 'Imperial' was released, gaining some more modest reviews. Unfortunately, that was more than could be said for the disappointing début album, originally to be eponymous, but finally titled *Sonic Flower Groove*. The record was a mish-mash of styles, weakly produced and poorly constructed, awash with average Sixties psychedelia. The over-intricate material never worked, and there were even rumours that the band themselves tried to get their record company to scrap the release. The subsequent poorly attended tour did little to lift the poor sales, and the rising tensions with the band saw yet more peripheral personnel changes. These smaller splits pre-empted a much more serious divide when, in the winter, founder member Jim Beattie left. He quickly formed Spirea X, named after an instrumental B-side by the Primals. Spirea X pursued the early Byrds feel that Beattie had brought to Primal Scream, but to more extreme levels. This new act produced two critically acclaimed EPs and a strong début album, *Fireblade Skies*, before falling from the limelight.

With Beattie out of the band, Bobby was the central figure once more, and the revised line-up meant a new sound. Dispensing with the 12-string Byrds obsession of Beattie, Bobby and core members Andrew Innes and Robert Young developed a newer, harder rock sound, and played covers by bands such as The Ramones and The Sex Pistols. Visually Primal Scream had changed too - pitch black long hair and skin-tight trousers hinted at a definite move towards rock territory.

With their longer hair, and former Nico back-up players Toby Tomanov and Henry Olsen in the ranks, the Primals' on-the-road antics began to gather as much publicity as their still-mediocre musical output. Tales of excess and debauchery followed them around wherever they gigged, and the band themselves did little to deny this. Inspired by The New York Dolls, all the members of Primal Scream tried to emulate Johnny Thunders and his notoriously wild lifestyle. Robert Young was a particular fan of Thunders, and whereas previously he was quite static on stage, he now began

Looking back on these years in the *NME*, Bobby later recalled: "We just got on with living the same lifestyle even if we hadn't been in a band. I would, Robert would and Andrew would still have taken as many drugs and done the things we did. You should always be able to indulge yourself, you should always be free to do exactly what you want. It's just fucking England, it's really puritan, it's too uptight. It's not loose enough. It's much better to be loose. You can be loose but at the same time be moral. But British people are definitely too reserved. I think we're

Bobby was unrepentant with regard to the band's reputation for attracting groupies. "Part of that is, let's face it, I like girls, right? And sometimes, if you want to go and get a lot of girls, then you should go and get a lot of girls. If girls like you and you like girls, then there's no reason you shouldn't have sex with them. I don't think it's a big deal." Rumours continued to spread, and some even alleged it was Alan McGee who was spreading them! Whatever the truth, the whispered tales did little to harm Primal Scream's growing popularity and profile.

An MC5-influenced single, 'Ivy, Ivy, Ivy', heralded the release of the band's eponymous second album in September 1989. With its patchy guitar work and disappointing songs, this was received with no more warmth than their début. Heavily soaked in MC5/T Rex reference points, it failed to break free from its influences. In the light of the Primals' latter-day success, it has enjoyed some reappraisal; at the time, however, it stiffed.

The band hid their disappointment with more Bacchanalian antics on the road, but even here there were disappointments. The first gig featuring this line-up was at Manchester's Hacienda, but the club was only half full and the atmosphere was dire. Afterwards, the band were in despair, although the very next night they played a storming show in Leeds that revitalised their belief in what they were doing. Generally, however, the public and the music media maintained a steady indifference to

Bobby then relocated to Brighton to take time out and recharge his batteries. Unbeknownst to him, a phenomenon was about to sweep Britain that would

"Primal Scream never deserted rock 'n' roll - they just introduced it to some interesting new acquaintances."

The Face magazine

In the middle of 1988, "Acid House" music swept through the UK's clubland, drenching everyone in hypnotic beats and new-age drug culture. Many saw it as evolving from the musical mecca of Chicago, others said it hailed from Detroit, and laid the credit at the feet of Juan Atkins, Derrick May, Kevin Saunderson and other innovative DJs and musicians. Whatever its actual origins, the new minimalist Acid House had many musical cousins, but its mind-altering frequencies, relentless rhythms, unconventional structures and off-beat soundscapes imbued it with a weirdness and unorthodoxy all of its own.

The music soon crossed the Atlantic, and was introduced to Britain through the massive illegal warehouse parties that formed the foundation for what became known as 'rave'. With the so-called smart bars selling high-energy, strictly non-alcoholic, caffeine-full drinks to fuel the marathon dancing, the culture rapidly adopted a recycled hippy mantra, and its "love vibe" and benign communality created what came to be called "The Summer Of Love". The establishment did not like it one bit (*Top Of The Pops* even banned some "acid" tracks) nor did the authorities, but an attempt to criminalise the raves only served to increase their rebellious flavour, and hence their popularity. Anti-drug squads were set up to combat the phenomena, but for now the baggy jeans and long-haired 'ravers' ran free across the country. Pirate radio stations filtered new material out from under the noses of the media, and the sheer scale of some all-nighters (frequently running to tens of thousands of kids) meant that the authorities had little power to stop them.

Settled in Brighton, Bobby watched this latest scene with fascination. The Zap Club in town was a favourite hang-out for ravers, and Bobby soon began to immerse himself in the music and the drug culture surrounding this new movement. He told the *NME* of one incident in Brighton which he revelled in: "There's these 11 and 12-year-old skateboarders on acid. Two of them came past me the other day, and one's saying, 'It's much better on acid isn't it?" Imagine that, at 12 years old when you've got no fucking hang-ups and your mind's still fairly pure... You'd feel like you were the Silver Surfer... Fucking brilliant."

Obviously there were many critics of the culture, since there was an undeniable wave of drugs beneath it, but Bobby was undeterred by this. Indeed, he was positively outspoken, as this extract from the *NME* shows: "I think if you allow drugs to completely change your personality then you've got something wrong with you, definitely. I mean, drugs can enhance your environment, they can enhance a good night out. When I first took acid it reinforced a lot of things that I already believed, and y'know, drugs are a good thing. I think. I would definitely proselytise for drugs any time, because people who use drugs wrongly, y'know, that's their problem. If you've got a brain then you're OK with drugs, really. It's like a motor car, you can kill yourself with a car if you drive wrongly. Give people the choice, that's what I say. Don't infringe on anybody's personal liberties."

Bobby saw the arrival of this new wave of music as the first real musical upheaval since punk. Once again parents were terrified of where their kids were at night, and he loved it. Primal Scream frequently drove up to London to sample the best of the capital's rave clubs, one of which was called Shoom. One of the key DJs there was Andy Weatherall, who, to the band's surprise, told them he was a huge fan of their belittled second album, and even more of a fan of the band's live show. This was particularly surprising, as at this time Primal Scream gigs were largely indifferent and always alarmingly brief. Bobby once said: "There should be a mandatory time limit on all gigs.

After 35 or 40 minutes, you should be off. Rock 'n' roll should be short, sharp and exciting. Too many bands just go on and on and on...." (Primal Scream regularly played ten minute gigs in their early days!).

Weatherall published the *Boys Own* fanzine about football and music and even reviewed one of Primal Scream's gigs for the *NME* under the pseudonym of Audrey Witherspoon! The two camps got on like a house on fire.

One track from the second album that Weatherall particularly liked was 'I'm Losing More Than I'll Ever Have'. He got hold of a tape from Innes, and took it back to re-mix, even though he had never done such a thing before in his career. Reborn, the track took the rock roots of Primal Scream and merged them with the incredible vibe of the rave scene into one mammoth tune. The furore that followed changed Primal Scream's career forever.

Weatherall had completely changed the track. He ripped out most of its soul and replaced it with a Soul II Soul-style drum beat (actually taken from a bootleg Eddie Brickell track), inserting a snippet of Peter Fonda saying "We wanna get loaded, and we wanna have a good time", from Roger Corman's infamous 1967 cult movie *The Wild Angels*. Bobby's vocals were almost entirely removed. To finish off what was effectively a complete, and virtually unrecognisable reconstruction, Weatherall also re-titled the track 'Loaded'.

[Incidentally, the Peter Fonda sample has an interesting background... Primal Scream's record company were worried that Fonda might sue over the use of the sample, so they insisted that the band tried to contact him for permission. Fonda had for some time been living in total seclusion and was rarely in contact with the outside world. Fortunately, an executive at the label knew Jane Fonda, so he put in a good word, and Jane duly travelled out to see Peter and played him the tape of the Primal Scream track. The band waited with baited breath for his response, and were delighted with the reply. "It's cool!" said Fonda who, after all, used to hang out with The Byrds. All he asked for was one penny per copy.]

Within weeks, Primal Scream were rocketed on to the mainstream stage. The single went gold in days, and a high chart entry and subsequent *Top Of The Pops* performance followed (rumours claimed the band had made full and unreserved use of the Beeb's rather generous rider - to some, Bobby seemed almost barely able to stand up). Suddenly, the media were hailing Primal Scream as the leaders of the so-called "indie/dance crossover", a battle between two previously opposite schools of thought. While EMF and Jesus Jones took this fusion to a more pop level, Primal Scream were winning all the critical plaudits for a similar merging of styles. Odd, then, that this was the result of an outsider's almost complete overhaul of their actual sound.

Realising their success was due to Weatherall's remix, and totally fascinated by the now ubiquitous yet underground dance scene, Primal Scream took this ethos on board wholeheartedly and immersed their music with a new dance core. Live shows to support the 'Loaded' single were filled with samplers, dance beats and drum machines. Suddenly, from being a predominantly retro rock band harping on about the Sixties, Primal Scream were at the very forefront of the newest musical hybrid.

In the wake of 'Loaded', dozens of bandwagon-jumping indie bands tried to mimic the stoned acid house swagger with far less success, and Primal Scream were subjected to criticism from certain detractors. Some said they had betrayed their rock past, while others claimed that in being virtually remixed off the track completely, the band were merely enjoying the fruits of someone else's talent. 808 State said they had betrayed their indie past, and for a few weeks there raged an argument (from which Primal Scream kept a dignified distance) about the relative merits of indie and dance and whether the two could ever be fused successfully). The dishevelled *Top Of The Pops* appearance for the single seemed to fuel stories that the Primals were getting off easily. Bobby was not interested. "From the very start we used to say that we liked Chic, we liked The Sex Pistols, we liked Sly Stone," he told the *NME*. "We've always been into that kind of stuff. Andrew, for instance, used to go to northern soul nights, take tons of speed and stay out all night dancing. I don't need to prove what I'm into to anybody."

As for the accusations that they weren't really on the record themselves, Bobby told the *NME*: "But it is our record. It's me that's singing on it. It's us playing guitars and bass. It's us that arranged it, arranged the gospel singers. OK, we hand the tapes over to Andy and he comes up with something completely different, but that's the whole point of it. We don't want it to be a slightly different version, we want him to take it somewhere else, completely out of this world."

To reinforce their belief in this new gospel, and to throw two fingers to their detractors, Primal Scream released their second, equally highly revered, single of the year, 'Come Together' - the 1990 summer anthem and another Top 30 hit. Although the signs of their Rolling Stones fixation were still there, this was a clear example of the Scream's new focus.

Compete with gospel choir and brass section, the track was another classic, although it didn't sell quite as heavily as the 200,000 copies that 'Loaded' had shifted. The brace of hits was expanded to a trio in June of 1991 with the third of a blistering set of singles, 'Higher Than The Sun', which included contributions from punk godfather Jah Wobble and The Orb's Alex Patterson. Alan McGee even went as far as to declare that 'Higher Than The Sun' was an 'Anarchy In The UK' for the Nineties, while the Creation press release claimed it was hallucinogenic space blues.

Bobby was quite open about his delight at charting, an attitude not necessarily in vogue with certain indie stars who saw the mainstream charts as a sell-out. Bobby told Ann Scanlon in *Sounds* : "We've always wanted to be on *Top Of The Pops* and be totally massive. That's why we always used to get upset when people called us an indie band, 'cos all the other bands who were round at the same time as us always looked really dour and drab and kinda ugly as well, and proud to be on an independent label. But if you look at any of our old interviews, we always said that we wanted to be a massive pop band."

More live dates and the arrival of a new member, Martin Duffy (formerly of Felt), strengthened their improving gigs. Their first female recruit, the sultry and soulful Denise Johnson, gave them yet another string to their bow. At last their live shows were beginning to match up to their records. A European tour in January 1990 was allegedly a speed-fuelled blitz through small and large clubs alike, with the media hungry for outrage and the band, as ever, fully equipped to provide it. One story claimed that Bobby and a crew member were so desperate to score some drugs that they wandered into a French chemists and pleaded with him to believe that the extremely potent medication they were asking for was for their weight problem, even though neither of them weighed more than ten stone! The tour bus rang to the sounds of MC5, The Impressions or even Aretha Franklin, while the shows were shambolically brilliant.

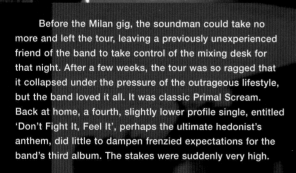

Before the Milan gig, the soundman could take no more and left the tour, leaving a previously unexperienced friend of the band to take control of the mixing desk for that night. After a few weeks, the tour was so ragged that it collapsed under the pressure of the outrageous lifestyle, but the band loved it all. It was classic Primal Scream. Back at home, a fourth, slightly lower profile single, entitled 'Don't Fight It, Feel It', perhaps the ultimate hedonist's anthem, did little to dampen frenzied expectations for the band's third album. The stakes were suddenly very high.

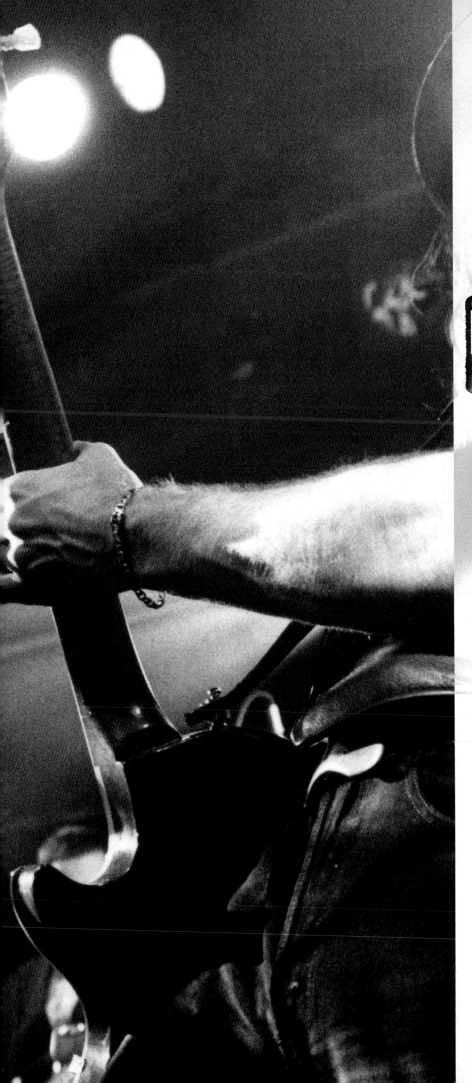

Chapter Four

"You know what they say?
Behind every great song there's a great pill."
Bobby Gillespie

The sessions for the third album were typically unpredictable. Bobby stayed with a friend in a small flat above some railway tracks, sharing a single bed for fitful sleep as the trains rushed by underneath, shaking the room to its foundations. He spent hours listening to records and each morning before heading off for the studio, he would play 'The Most Beautiful Girl' by Charlie Rich and 'I'm Stone In Love With You' by The Stylistics.

Lyrically, Bobby explained his focus thus: "I think a lot of the songs are about things that you love that you can't have - it's unresolved. You kinda know how the world should be but it isn't and it never will be that way 'cos of the way that the world's set up, and all these things come into my mind when I write lyrics." For two tracks, 'Movin' On Up' and 'Damaged', the Primals were mixed by Jimmy Miller, who had been behind the mixing desk for The Stones' classic albums *Let It Bleed* and *Sticky Fingers*. Their Stones fixation had now finally come full circle.

Despite the success of the two singles, Bobby was still apprehensive about how the new record would be received. "Last year most people hated our group, apart from Andy Weatherall... but the group believed in itself so much that we just kept going and going and going. That's the kind of people we are. So, this year, if nobody likes us and we think what we're doing is great it would be kinda hurtful, but so what?"

He needn't have worried. When the history of music for the Nineties is written, Primal Scream's third album, *Screamadelica*, will be placed firmly near the top (if not at the top) of the greatest albums of that decade. With material that had been written over 18 months, and soaked in the rave and dance culture, the record was almost immediately acknowledged as a modern classic. It brought together those four remarkable singles, and threw in yet more equally stunning tracks. It covered all bases, and everyone seemed to love it.

The critical response was well upbeat. It easily consolidated the success of the preceding singles, and its seismic impact on British music is still being felt to this day. The record was a Top Ten smash, and sales remained massive for months to come. The *NME* called it "masterful" and *Select* magazine made it their album of the year, and said it was the best album of the decade thus far. A batch of similar plaudits followed as the end of year polls flooded in. The final recognition of the work's quality came when the first ever Mercury Music Award was given to Primal Scream for that album, along with a £25,000 first prize.

Bobby was not about to argue. In the wake of the Madchester scene, he cheekily laid claim to having started the whole phenomenon, telling *Sounds*: "A lot of kids who are into The Stone Roses and The Charlatans are listening to our first album and loving it. That album is like a precursor to a sound that's quite popular these days. We made that three years ago and, in a way, it's all kind of come back to us 'cos three years ago nobody liked us either. If we'd been a new band and released that album last year, we'd have been huge. But that's the way pop music goes - you've got to be in the right place at the right time and I appreciate that 'cos I love pop music."

The most retro track on the album, 'Movin' On Up', was chosen as the next single, where it lead the so-called *Dixie-Narco* EP in January 1992. Recorded in Memphis at the same Ardent Studios that were used by Big Star (whose music, and third album *3rd* in particular, were a massive influence on Primal Scream), the EP enjoyed great success in the UK. On the B-side was a ten-minute disco mantra with the same title as the album, as well as a scary version of Dennis Wilson's 'Carry Me Home'. The excellent package was rewarded when it became the Scream's first ever Top Ten hit single. Another loaded appearance on *Top Of The Pops* confirmed that 1992 was their year.

Touring *Screamadelica* was another epic Primals experience. A stunning series of all-night shows opened with The Orb's Dr Alex Patterson spinning the decks, before the band played and then Andy Weatherall closed the evening's proceedings. There were no support acts, and at the close of the night the punters filed out of the hall to the sound of Sly And The Family Stone and MC5. Bobby explained his philosophy towards touring and the challenges of reproducing the complex new sound on stage: "Our group's always been a group that's stopped playing for a year until we've got a whole new set. It's gonna be a different sound - more electro, but at the same time with heavy guitars. Now we can do stuff like having backward strings, congas and percussion." He also looked forward to the coming US dates, saying "We're doing 'Frisco, LA and San Diego - basically it's just ten days of getting wasted. McGee's coming and other sundry nutcases are gonna make their way over too. So I want us to get a whole floor at the Hyatt, where Led Zeppelin used to stay."

America: this was the one territory that the all-conquering album failed to set alight. With the almost complete absence of any mainstream success for the rave scene in the US, where dance music constantly struggled with the MOR-dominated radio and charts, the Scream enjoyed little success across the Atlantic. This did little to dampen their spirits back in the UK, where Bobby's band were king. But for Primal Scream, the US was the spiritual home of many of their influences. The blues, soul and so much of American culture were the very basis of the band's existence. To add to that, they were really looking forward to the trip: "I think our music will go down really well in America, for a start," Bobby told the media. "You see, a lot of really bad British bands have kind of half-made it in America and you just think, 'Well, what are they going to do when they hear us?' 'cos we're so good. Also, I'd quite like to see what America does to some of the people in our band. I'd like to see how people cope with it, and I include myself in that... It appeals to my sense of humour. Basically, someone's not going to come back America... There'll be some good stories to tell." Despite Primal Scream's excitement about these dates, and the fact that they did indeed "get wasted for ten days", the tiny size of the tour and the muted impact of 'Loaded' on the *Billboard* charts meant that this jaunt did little to penetrate the otherwise impervious American market. Fortunately, the same could not be said of Japan, where the dates were sold out and the reaction from the crowd ecstatic.

On their return to the UK, after a handful of yet more dates, including a show-stopping performance at the Glastonbury Festival in 1992, and a slot appearing with The Orb at the Miners' Benefit in Sheffield the same year, Primal Scream went to ground and didn't re-emerge for a full two years.

Chapter Five

"They were doing some mixing and they looked
more focused than I'd ever seen them.

They both had that giveaway glint in the eye

that you only get when you are
right on the fucking case."

Irvine Welsh

The making of Primal Scream's fourth album is a story
in itself. The pressure of producing an appropriately strong
follow-up to the universally acclaimed *Screamadelica*
was immense from the offset. Many locations and names
were discussed, but eventually the band opted to record
in Memphis, at the aforementioned Ardent Studios.
At the helm this time were Roger Hawkins, David Hood
and Tom Dowd, (who between them had worked with
Otis Redding, Aretha Franklin, Wilson Pickett, Rod Stewart,
Percy Sledge, Donnie Fritts and James Carr).
Initial rehearsals took place in London and all the
early signs were good. Such was the respect the band had
for these people that they were playing out of their skins.

コンパニオン募集 !!
六本木 **クリスタル**
☎3583-8217

When the sprightly 70-year-old Dowd arrived the sessions really began to liven up. Dowd disciplined the band, not something they were previously used to, and took control of the recordings. Relocating to Muscle Shoals in northern Alabama, the band knuckled down to work. Oddly, the town shuts down at 9pm, so for once there were few extra-curricular distractions to lure them away from their main task. Also making appearances on the record were Jim Dickinson (who contributed piano to the Osmonds classic 'Crazy Horses' and was a one-time Stones and Big Star collaborator), George Clinton of Parliament fame, Benmont Tench (Heartbreakers), and George Drakoulias of Black Crowes fame. Clinton ended up mixing three tracks on the album and actually sang on two tracks as well. At the tail end of the year Primal Scream flew back out to America, this time to Los Angeles, to re-record a couple of tracks that hadn't quite worked, especially 'Call On Me'.

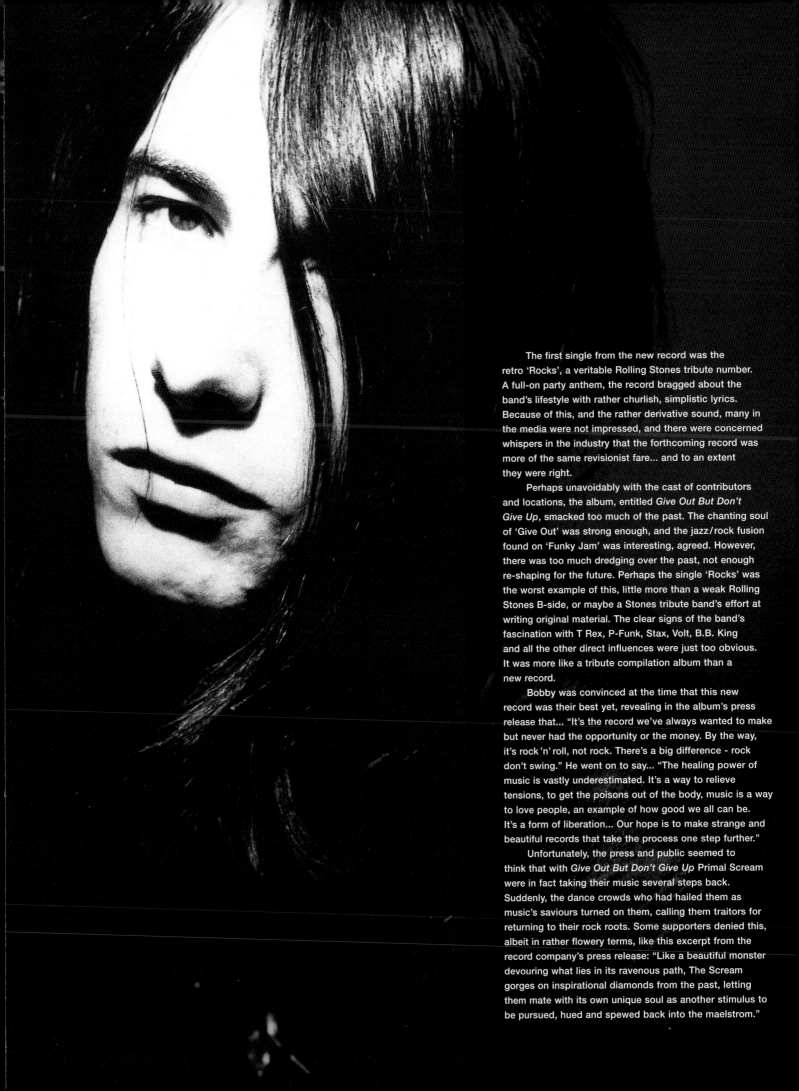

The first single from the new record was the retro 'Rocks', a veritable Rolling Stones tribute number. A full-on party anthem, the record bragged about the band's lifestyle with rather churlish, simplistic lyrics. Because of this, and the rather derivative sound, many in the media were not impressed, and there were concerned whispers in the industry that the forthcoming record was more of the same revisionist fare... and to an extent they were right.

Perhaps unavoidably with the cast of contributors and locations, the album, entitled *Give Out But Don't Give Up*, smacked too much of the past. The chanting soul of 'Give Out' was strong enough, and the jazz/rock fusion found on 'Funky Jam' was interesting, agreed. However, there was too much dredging over the past, not enough re-shaping for the future. Perhaps the single 'Rocks' was the worst example of this, little more than a weak Rolling Stones B-side, or maybe a Stones tribute band's effort at writing original material. The clear signs of the band's fascination with T Rex, P-Funk, Stax, Volt, B.B. King and all the other direct influences were just too obvious. It was more like a tribute compilation album than a new record.

Bobby was convinced at the time that this new record was their best yet, revealing in the album's press release that... "It's the record we've always wanted to make but never had the opportunity or the money. By the way, it's rock 'n' roll, not rock. There's a big difference - rock don't swing." He went on to say... "The healing power of music is vastly underestimated. It's a way to relieve tensions, to get the poisons out of the body, music is a way to love people, an example of how good we all can be. It's a form of liberation... Our hope is to make strange and beautiful records that take the process one step further."

Unfortunately, the press and public seemed to think that with *Give Out But Don't Give Up* Primal Scream were in fact taking their music several steps back. Suddenly, the dance crowds who had hailed them as music's saviours turned on them, calling them traitors for returning to their rock roots. Some supporters denied this, albeit in rather flowery terms, like this excerpt from the record company's press release: "Like a beautiful monster devouring what lies in its ravenous path, The Scream gorges on inspirational diamonds from the past, letting them mate with its own unique soul as another stimulus to be pursued, hued and spewed back into the maelstrom."

In the hope that their much-criticised album might come to life on the road, Primal Scream took to the tour bus for a gruelling year long slew of international dates. The headline slot at the Reading Festival was well received, and buoyed their already faltering confidence, after which they joined the equally rock 'n' roll Depeche Mode for a support slot on their mammoth arena tour. During these dates, outrageous tales of ridiculous excess were circulated, understandably when two such excessive bands collided, but Bobby later played this down, calling the tour "death by boredom". He was particularly worried by the megastar lifestyle to which the globally successful Depeche Mode succumbed: "(They) are really good guys... but it was four separate dressing rooms, four separate limousines, four separate hotel suites. I couldn't do that." This down-to-earth mentality was partly born of his working-class background - his father was a trade union official and Bobby himself was a staunch left-wing socialist. At the advent of New Labour, Bobby announced he was disappointed with their new agenda and would be voting for the far more left-wing socialist party of Arthur Scargill.

Dates in Australia with Ministry and Hole were followed by a triumphant British tour, this time supported by Andrew Weatherall's Sabres Of Paradise, The Chemical Brothers and Kris Needs DJing every night. To some extent, their hopes that the average album would spring to life on tour were justified. The rather staid rock record did sound better on stage, and the band's infamously hedonistic approach to touring seemed to inject a vibrancy that was lacking on record. Perhaps the best date of the entire marathon was the Brixton Academy show at the tail end of 1994, when they were joined on stage by George Clinton and a twenty-piece Funkadelic Orchestra. Despite these highlights, the ticket sales were only average, record sales poor, and morale on the road constantly at a low. With the soul-destroying world tour over, the band were nearly on the verge of splitting up.

By the time they staggered, battered, out of 1994, a lengthy lay-off period was called for to recharge their batteries. Shortly into this lay-off, Bobby was admitting to himself that he too disliked the album. In an admirably open interview with the *NME*, he opened up to his reservations about the record: "I saw some pictures of me towards the end last time... I just didn't give a fuck! I let myself go.

Clothes, hair, personal hygiene. I just didn't give a fuck! I didn't get depressed about it until six months after it came out. You know, it was sounding great live... but six months later I realised it wasn't what it should've been. I was thinking seriously of splitting the band up. Because if we couldn't be as good as I knew we could be, if we were only going to be alright instead of... Primal Scream, I couldn't see any point in carrying on. One day you wake up and look in the mirror and your hair's down to your arse and you look like a goddamn hippy! That's when you think, 'Oh fuck! Let's review the situation!' (The album) was over-produced, too clean. It should've sounded late-night, mournful, but still uplifting. Dirtier and darker. '(I'm Gonna) Cry Myself Blind', 'Rocks': they're good, but some of the other stuff... when we wrote the album we were kind of fucked, but the album never reflected that, unfortunately. We were bruised and broken, but that album never captured it."

Chapter Six

"The drug culture in England is so heavy right now.
And we're no different than anyone else here.

But it's getting out of control."
Bobby Gillespie

The first sign of Primal Scream's emergence from their lengthy sabbatical was in February 1996, when they contributed a superb instrumental to the classic Irvine Welsh film *Trainspotting*. Having met Welsh when he was sent to interview them for *i-D* magazine, the band and writer got on famously - he loved their music and irreverent rock 'n' roll lifestyle, they loved his writing (*Acid House* had just been published when they first met). As Primals keyboardist Martin Duffy put it to journalist Dave Kendall, "He just came to interview us, and we just clicked with him, you know? We've just been going out on the piss with him ever since. Good bloke."

Then their first single in two years was released, a collaboration with Welsh and dub DJ Adrian Sherwood, entitled 'The Big Man & The Scream Team Meet The Barmy Army Uptown'. Released for only one week, it was aimed to coincide with the start of the Euro '96 football championships, in particular the highly charged clash between Scotland and England. The single sold out completely before it was deleted after seven days. The clever mix of football chant-style vocals and brilliant musical backdrop reasserted the Primals' belief in what they were doing.

For most of the rest of the year, Primal Scream were holed up in their own tiny recording studio in Chalk Farm, north London. Devoid of windows, the shabby room had old Airfix models hanging from the ceilings and only a sprinkling of equipment, much of which had seen better days. Mixed in with this was some state of the art technology, including two portable eight-track recording studios. The walls were covered in the week's main headlines, hastily cut from the tabloids, and cigarette smoke hung thickly in the air as there was no ventilation. The most productive sessions in this rather claustrophobic environment came during the summer heatwave, when a diverse and rich tapestry of styles began to form, including dub, soul, rock, punk and even metal. Andrew Innes engineered and programmed the entire record, then Paul Weller's producer Brendan Lynch moved in for post-production and mixing. The session moved quickly - in three months it was all virtually complete.

Despite this more disciplined approach, Bobby explained to the *NME* that the recording process was never sterile: "This time there were no rules and it was exciting and electric. We captured the moment, it was all one take and then get to fuck! It's live playing with Innes putting weird hallucinogenic stuff over it. We made the album straight, but I'd really like to hear it on acid. I bet it would sound incredible. We stand for experimentation again. High-energy rock 'n' roll. Psychedelic experimentation and punk music. We wanted to excite ourselves as well as everyone else and we have."
This fluidity also applied to the seamless track choice, which on the surface appeared very deliberate: "The order was completely spontaneous, the songs just happened to be put together like this. It's incredible. We never think things out. We just do it! I wish I could say we planned it."

Vanishing Point carries a litany of top names. Alongside the core Primals personnel were The Memphis Horns, former Sex Pistol Glen Matlock, Marco Nelson and old friend Andrew Weatherall. Then, at the tail end of these sessions, the former Stone Roses bassist and motormouth Gary 'Mani' Mountfield joined the Primals, perhaps making them a latterday supergroup. He was not about to let this opportunity slip by, as he told the *NME*: "98% was done. Man was already walking erect from the first amoeba that slid out of the sea by the time I got involved in the LP, you know what I mean? I just came down and played on the single and a few of the B-sides. So now I'm like a salesman, I've got a stout foot in the door. And now I'm gonna close the deal." His eclectic style and musical knowledge, along with his effervescent character, were an ideal catalyst for the band to satisfactorily complete the album on time. Mani himself was delighted to have been recruited, saying in the *NME*: "I've come home to my real family, the Roses were my foster family. I've always felt kinship with Bobby, he's an inspirational leader and good socialist - '96 was a shit year for me, bands breaking up, relationships breaking up... but '97 really feels right How couldn't it? I'm in the best band in the world."

Taking its name from Richard Sarafin's 1971 speed-fuelled cult movie, *Vanishing Point* was the Primals' fifth album and a thunderous return to form. The main character of this famous movie was a car delivery driver called Kowalski, whose name provided the title of a future Primals single. The rumbling bass lines and groove-riddled melodies laced the album with a contemporary and vibrant feel that was sorely lacking on the previous album. Tracks like the excellent ballad 'Star' mixed beautifully with the more punk rock noise of 'Medication'. There was even room for metal, with 'Motorhead', breakbeat funk with 'If They Move, Kill 'Em' and dub/classical with 'Stuka'. The opening 'Burning Wheel' was very Syd Barrett, and all across the record synths mixed with guitar effects, reverb and strange drum loops. It was complex, direct and stunning. Primal Scream were back in business.

A key motivation for the album was to provide a harder, more appropriate soundtrack to *Vanishing Point* than the rather insipid hippie music that originally accompanied it. Lyrically, some of the album reflected the dark focus of the road movie, but there was also a sinister insinuation, quite direct at times, about Bobby's rumoured dalliances with harder drugs, heroin in particular. In the *NME*, he was clearly uneasy about discussing this in depth: "Oh, right, aye, that. Mmmm... it's all there in the lyrics. I don't want to say anything too dumb... it's a dark record but I've found redemption. There's things that've happened to us. You don't need me to fill in the gaps, and I don't want to... There are horror stories I could tell you, but I don't want to get into horror stories... I think with the lyrics I'm trying to tell you what I've seen, what I feel and how it is. That's as specific as I'm going to get... I don't know... I really don't want to go into it."

Despite this dangerous subject matter, Bobby was brimming with confidence for the new record, saying in the press: "I think this album is better than *Screamadelica*, much better. I love *Screamadelica*, but I think *Vanishing Point* is a pure Primal Scream album. I think we've really truly found our voice." When asked if he thought people would buy this new album he told *Select*: "I don't know. If they don't, they don't . We love it. We're proud of it. I played a couple of tracks to a pal of mine and he says 'The Scream are the Total Football of music. Ajax '74, Johnny Rep, Neeskens and Cruyff' - that's good enough for me."

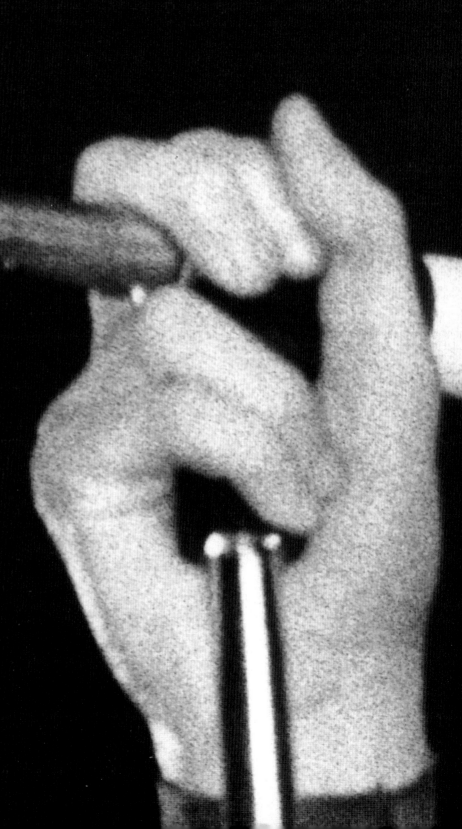

The press agreed. On its release in July 1997, the critical applause was warm and widespread, with an audible sigh of relief that one of Britain's mightier bands had returned to form. *Melody Maker enthused* "In a laudable (and typically Scream-like) gesture of defiance, they've staged one of the most audacious and spectacular comebacks of recent memory. *Vanishing Point* re-defines the band's parameters, giving them an edge and a hunger that none of their other albums... ever had. It's restless, alive and driven, continuously striving to push styles and genres to their limits, putting square pegs into round holes, fucking around with everything from psychedelia to punk and dub to funk. It's the sound of a band whole-heartedly embracing the limitless potential of music. It's cold and alien; a menace, madness, totally out of control", while writer Dave Kendall summed it up as "a dissociated grab bag of goodies, greaties and mediocrities, with no consistency, shape or focus. It is truly a stream of (altered) consciousness."

Critics had dogged Primal Scream's entire career, and the new album was no different. Those narrow-minded and ill-educated enough to ignore the band's turn-of-the decade masterpiece accused the Primals of bandwagon-jumping on to the dance floor. Bobby dealt with these accusations with suitable contempt: "I don't care what people think," he told *The Times*, "Fuck 'em. We'll be here and then we'll be gone, and if we touch some people... then, fair enough. Anyway, house music was first invented in the States in places like Chicago and Detroit, but it goes back to German groups like Kraftwerk, Can, Neu and Cluster in the Seventies... (with *Screamadelica*) we were at least six years ahead of our time."

At least the album launch had its fair share of classic Primal Scream rock tales: one rumoured story related the tale of how, at an exclusive American album party, Bobby was looking around the palatial home of the record company executive who was running the show. Asked what he thought of the glorious surroundings, Bobby replied: "I'd like to burn it down...", to which came the reply: "Oh, don't do that, I have many wonderful parties here." The executive then jokingly quipped "How would you like to set fire to the swimming pool?" at which point Bobby fixed him with a stare and said: "You got any gasoline?"

A still better story surrounded the release of the single 'Kowalski'. At the Paul Weller launch party for his new album Heavy Soul, the assembled VIPs were played a sample of the ModFather's new record and applauded politely. Then, allegedly, a rather drunken Bobby Gillespie pushed a video tape into the player and screened Primal Scream's forthcoming video for the new single 'Kowalski'. The Irvine Welsh scripted picture showed extreme violence and recklessness as two female heavies are sent to kill the band. The clip is a bizarre mix of *Natural Born Killers* and *Faster Pussy Cat Kill Kill*. The screen went blank and apparently there was total silence. Stunned silence. Bobby and Primal Scream had stolen the show.

Taking its name from the film's central character, Kowalski, the single offers a musical backdrop to the high-powered drive from Denver to San Francisco in under two days. All the while Kowalski is being chased by the police and various gangsters who are out to kill him, and along the way he consumes copious amounts of speed as he encounters a multitude of vicious scenarios. A DJ called Super Soul broadcasts messages of support during his journey, and it is this voice that is sampled for the single. It is a very punk film. Very seedy. Very Primal Scream.

Chapter Seven

"There's no reason for them to split.
They've just made their best album."

Bobby was very excited about the forthcoming album tour: "We'll use keyboards, synthesizers, drum loops and computer programs married with live musicians. It's gonna be real high-energy, but experimental and abstract as well." Unfortunately, however, the tour for *Vanishing Point* was dogged with difficulties, collapsing amidst a morass of hearsay and rumour.

Firstly, an unnamed member of the band had allegedly been sent to hospital to cure a nagging medical problem, fuelling rumours of narcotic excess once again. The band's spokesman refused to name the member, but said: "It's a health problem one of the band members has got. I can't go into it. It's not a drugs thing and it's not a nervous breakdown. It's like a personal thing which people get from time to time. Somebody has to go and get something done around the time of the gigs. It's something very basic which, hopefully, can be sorted out quite quickly by a trained doctor." He also emphatically denied that the band's future was in doubt. This last reassurance was in response to the rumours that the Primals were dogged by internal problems. Some allegations suggested that keyboard player Martin Duffy had walked out on the band, while others said he was tipped to join The Charlatans. "No one is leaving," retorted the Primals adamantly. Other rumours said Mani had left to re-join Ian Brown in his new group, but again the spokesman denied all reports. Another declared that guitarist Throb had also left. On this matter the spokesman joked: "Duffy left the band in 1994, when he was replaced by a waxwork. I can't see any reason why he would leave. This is the first time he's had a writing credit, on this album!" He went on: "There's no reason for them to split. They've just made their best album. There's no one leaving. As soon as you cancel any gigs, unless you can give a cut and dried reason, like one of them has to have his leg removed, people do start to speculate."

Primal Scream's problems continued at the delayed Glasgow Green gig, Towards the end of their excellent set, an unknown assailant ran amok around the crowd stabbing people with a hypodermic syringe before escaping into the night. One fan tried to grab him, but had to let go when he was also stabbed; 14 other people needed treatement for stab wounds. The band issued a statement afterwards, urging fans to check themselves for puncture wounds, which in the heat and environment of a gig might have gone unnoticed, adding, "We are all collectively shocked and disturbed by this sick, degraded behaviour and our thoughts are with the people who were hurt and their families." For this to happen at a hometown gig which was to have been a triumphant return after the difficult fourth album, made the nasty incident doubly unfortunate. A Glasgow Health Authority helpline set up to answer worried fans' questions received over 200 calls in a matter of days. The hospital denied that anyone was likely to have caught HIV from the attack, although many did have preventative Hepatitis B vaccinations and counselling.

In the light of these difficulties, the band derailed any plans to tour the US, meaning that it was now three years since they had last travelled around the States on the Depeche Mode tour. Bobby is adamant that if they do finally tour the US next year it will be on their own terms, telling *The Times*... "That's what's good about this band, we take chances. We want to be like The Velvet Underground or The Stooges. A band that, when people look back, they'll say, in the context of what was going on in '97, 'They made some crazy records... But they were great.' On the singles front, the excellent 'Burning Wheel' single showcased a The Chemical Brothers remix, and gave the Primals an autumn Top 20 hit. Then in October came a remixed version of the *Vanishing Point* album, entitled *Echo Dek*, featuring new versions of tracks by esteemed studio wizards such as Adrian Sherwood.

Despite his more mature years, and the reported difficulties he has had with drug abuse, Bobby's attitude to this lifestyle seems undeterred. In late 1997, he openly discussed his feelings on drugs in *The Times*, and it seemed clear he had few regrets: "Today, there's a lot more heroin and cocaine than there ever was in Great Britain. There's a population of 55 million and I think two or three million Ecstasy tablets are sold every weekend. It's insane. Most of the songs are influenced by our imaginations. We don't always need drugs to make music, ya know... I do like dexedrines, though. Purely pharmaceutical. I've got a scrip so they're legal."

Conclusion

In early 1998, Primal Scream have already started work on their next album. Once again they have invited numerous illustrious collaborators along for the ride, including Can drummer Jaki Leibezeit and My Bloody Valentine mainman Kevin Shields, as well as, remarkably, Liam Gallagher who plays piano on one track. They have also started work on another Irvine Welsh film project, an adaptation of *The Acid House*, for which they will contribute a new track. Furthermore, Bobby told *Addicted To Noise* Internet fanzine that they had also recorded a cover version of garage band Fifth Bardo's 'I'm Five Years Ahead of My Time', again with Kevin Shields, which he said sounded like "a squadron of jet fighters". There are even rumours that the writing is going so well, the new album will be out by late summer '98.

Despite everything that has happened to Primal Scream, the critical attacks, the personal and personnel problems, and the lengthy lay-offs, they still remain one of the shining lights of British music. And at the very centre of this beacon is Bobby (voted the 65th Most Important Man in the World by *Select* magazine!). Maybe it is this that has kept them together and kept them so creative. If his motivations for making music are anything to go by then Primal Scream will be around for a very long time to come: "Basically I just want to prove how great music can be - how it can affect people spiritually, how it can heal people. I want to show how beautiful it can be, how tragic it can be. Everything music does for me, I want to do for other people. I mean, I think there's a lot of great records about - I'm not one of these people who thinks all the great pop music was done in 1967 - but a lot of records are only good up to a point, they don't completely seduce me. I want to completely seduce people with our music - I want their hearts to break when they hear it."

Discography

Singles

All Fall Down
All Fall Down
It Happens

May '85
7" UK Creation CRE 017

Crystal Crescent
Crystal Crescent
Velocity Girl
Spirea X

May '86
7" UK Creation CRE 026
12" UK Creation CRE 026T

Gentle Tuesday
Gentle Tuesday
Black Star Carnival
I'm Gonna Make You Mine

June '87
7" UK Elevation ACID 3
12" UK Elevation ACID 3T

Imperial
Imperial
Star Fruit Surf Rider
So Sad About Us
Imperial (Demo Version)

September '87
7" UK Elevation ACID 5
12" UK Elevation ACID 5T
12" UK Elevation ACID 5TW

Ivy Ivy Ivy
Ivy Ivy Ivy
You're Just Too Dark To Care
I Got You Split Wide Open Over Me

July '89
7" UK Creation CRE 067
12" UK Creation CRE 067T
CD5 UK Creation CRESCD 067

Loaded
Loaded
I'm Losing More Than I'll Ever Have
Ramblin' Rose (Live in NYC)

February '90
7" UK Creation CRE 070
12" UK Creation CRE 070T
CD5 UK Creation CRESCD 070

Come Together
Come Together (Terry Farley Mix)
Come Together
   (Andy Weatherall Mix)

August '90
7" UK Creation CRE 078
MC UK Creation CRECS 078
12" UK Creation CRE 078T
CD5 UK Creation CRESCD 078

Higher Than The Sun
Higher Than The Sun (7" Mix)
Higher Than The Sun
   (American Spring Mix)
Higher Than The Sun
   (Higher Than The Orb)

June '91
7" UK Creation CRE 096
CD5 UK Creation CRESCD 096
12" UK Creation CRE 096T

Don't Fight It, Feel It
Don't Fight It, Feel It (7" Edit)
Don't Fight It, Feel It (12" Version)
Don't Fight It, Feel It (Scat Mix)

August '91
7" UK Creation CRE 110
12" UK Creation CRE 110T
CD5 UK Creation CRESCD 110

Dixie-Narco EP
Movin' On Up
Stone My Soul
Carry Me Home
Screamadelica

January '92
7" UK Creation CRE 117
12" UK Creation CRE 117T
CD5 UK Creation CRESCD 117
MC UK Creation CRE 117

Movin' On Up
Movin' On Up
Screamadelica

February '92
12" Creation CRE117TP

Slip Inside This House
Slip Inside This House
Loaded
Higher Than The Sun
   (American Spring Mix)
You're Just Too Dark To Care

March '92
CD5 AUS Columbia

Rocks
Rocks
Funky Jam (Hot Ass Mix)
Funky Jam (Club Mix)

February '94
7" UK Creation CRE 129
12" UK Creation CRE 129T
CD5 UK Creation CRESCD 129
CD5 Europe Sony 660096-2

Jailbird
Jailbird (The Original Mix)
Jailbird (The Dust Brothers Mix)
Jailbird (The Toxic Trio Stay
   Free Mix)
Jailbird (Sweeney 2 Mix)
Jailbird (Weatherall Dub
   Chapter 3 Mix)

June '94
7" UK Creation CRE 145
12" UK Creation CRE 145T
CD5 UK Creation CRESCD 145
MC UK Creation CRECS 145

(I'm Gonna) Cry Myself Blind
(I'm Gonna) Cry Myself Blind
Rocks (Live)
I'm Losing More Than I'll
   Ever Have (Live)
Struttin' (Back In Our Minds)
Live at Glasgow Barrowlands '94

November '94
7" UK Creation CRE 183
CD5 UK Creation CRESCCD 183 Promo
CD5 UK Creation CRESCD 183
MC UK Creation CRE 183
CD5 Europe Sony 660687-2

**Primal Scream, Irvine Welsh
and On-U-Sound present...
The Big Man and the Scream
Team Meet The Barmy Army
Uptown**
Full Strength Fortified Dub
Electric Soup Dub
A Jake Supreme

June '96
12" UK Creation CRE194T
CD5 UK Creation CRESCD194
MC UK Creation CRE194

Kowalski
Kowalski
Know Your Rights (Clash)
96 Tears (Question Mark &
   The Mysterions)
Kowalski (Automator Mix) DT

May '97
7" UK Creation CRE245
12" UK Creation CRE245T
CD5 UK Creation CRESCD245

Star
Star
Jesus
Rebel Dub
How Does It Feel To Belong

June '97
7" UK Creation CRE263
10" UK Creation CRE263X
12" UK Creation CRE263T
12" UK Creation CRE263TP (Promo)
CD5 UK Creation CRESCD263
CD5 UK Creation CRESCD263P (Promo)

Stuka
Stuka (Two Lone Swordsman Mix)
Stuka (Two Lone Swordsman
   Instrumental Mix)

September '97
12" UK Creation PSTLS1

Burning Wheel
Burning Wheel
Burning Wheel
   (Chemical Brothers Mix)
Hammond Connection
Higher Than The Sun

October '97
7" UK Creation CRE 272
12" UK Creation CRE 272T
CD5 UK Creation CRESCD 272

If They Move, Kill 'Em
If They Move, Kill 'Em
   (Original Mix)
If They Move, Kill 'Em
   (Kevin Shield Mix)
If They Move, Kill 'Em
   (Rave & Christian mix)
If They Move, Kill 'Em
   (Skylab mix)

February '98
7" UK Creation CRE 284
12" UK Creation CRE 284T
CD5 UK Creation CRESCD 284

Albums

Sonic Flower Groove
Gentle Tuesday
Treasure Trip
May The Sun Shine Bright For You
Sonic Sister Love
Silent Spring
Imperial
Love You
Leaves
Aftermath
We Go Down Slowly Rising

(September '87)
LP UK Elevation ELV 2
CD Europe Warner 242182-2
(re-release '91)
Produced by Mayo Thompson
All songs written by Beattie, Gillespie

Primal Scream
Ivy Ivy Ivy
You're Just Dead Skin To Me
She Power
You're Just Too Dark To Care
I'm Losing More Than
   I'll Ever Have
Gimme Gimme Teenage Head
Lone Star Girl
Kill The King
Sweet Pretty Thing
Jesus Can't Save Me

September '89
LP UK Creation CRELP 054
CD UK Creation CRECD 054
*Produced by Sister Anne
(Primal Scream)*
*All songs written by Gillespie,
Innes, Young*

Screamadelica
Movin' On Up
Slip Inside This House
Don't Fight It, Feel It
   (featuring Denise Johnson)
Higher Than The Sun
Inner Flight
Come Together
   (Andy Weatherall-Extended)
Loaded (Extended)
Damaged
I'm Coming Down
Higher Than The Sun -
   A Dub Symphony In Two Parts
   (featuring Jah Wobble)
Shine Like Stars

September '91
LP UK Creation CRELP 076
CD UK Creation CRECD 076P Promo
CD UK Creation CRECD 076
CD US Sire 2-26714
*Produced by Andrew Weatherall
and assisted by Hugo Nicholson for
Boys Own Productions*
*All songs written by Gillespie, Innes,
Young*

Give Out But Don't Give Up
Jailbird
Rocks
(I'm Gonna) Cry Myself Blind
Funky Jam
Big Jet Plane
Free
Call On Me
Struttin'
Sad And Blue
Give Out But Don't Give Up
I'll Be There For You
Everybody Needs Somebody
   (Hidden Bonus Track)

March '94
CD UK Creation CRECD 146P Promo
CD UK Creation CRECD 146
CD US Sire/Creation
LP UK Creation CRELP 146
Came with a print of Cover
*All songs written by Gillespie,
Innes, Young*

Vanishing Point
Burning Wheel
Get Duffy
Kowalski
Star
If They Move, Kill 'Em
Out Of The Void
Stuka
Medication
Motorhead
Trainspotting
Long life

July '97
CD UK Creation CRECD 178
CD US Sire/Creation
LP UK Creation CRELP 178
MC UK Creation CCRE 178
*Produced by Brendan Lynch and
Primal Scream*
*All songs written by Gillespie, Innes,
Young, Duffy except 'Kowalski'
by Gillespie, Innes, Young, Duffy
and Mountfield and 'Motorhead '
by Kilmister (Motorhead).*

Echo Dek
Living Dub (Long Life)
Duffed Up (Get Duffy)
Revolutionary (Star)
JU-87 (Stuka)
First Name Unknown (Kowalski)
Vain In Dub (Out Of The void)
Last Train (Trainspotting)
Wise Blood (Stuka)
Dub In Vain (Medication)

October '97
CD UK Creation CRECD 224
LP UK Creation CRELP 224P
7x5 UK Creation CRE 224
*Produced by Brendan Lynch and
Primal Scream*
Remixed by Adrian Sherwood
*All songs written by Gillespie,
Innes, Young, Duffy except 'Kowalski'
by Gillespie, Innes, Young, Duffy
and Mountfield*

Videos

Screamadelica
Screamadelica, Movin' On Up,
Slip Inside This House,
Don't Fight It, Feel It Higher
Than The Sun, Come Together,
Damaged, Loaded,
Shine Like Stars

1992
Video UK Creation / Virgin VVD1041
Laserdisc JAPAN / No Cat. No.

Credits

*There is an excellent Record
Collector article on the early days
of Primal Scream (issue 177).
Also, the following magazines were
of invaluable help in my research
and can provide superb sources for
Primal Scream fans: NME,
Melody Maker, Sounds, The Times,
Zig Zag, Select, Mojo, Vox, Q.*